Step by Step

T0011577

The Story of Bread

It Starts with Wheat

Stacy Taus-Bolstad

Lerner Publications ◆ Minneapolis

Lerner Publications Company
An imprint of Lerner Publishing Group, Inc.
241 First Avenue North
Minneapolis, MN 55401 USA

For reading levels and more information, look up this title at www.lernerbooks.com.

Image credits: Jose Luis Pelaez Inc/DigitalVision/Getty Images, p. 3; photolinc/Shutterstock.com, pp. 5, 23 (bottom right); USDA NRCS Montana/flickr (CC0), p. 7; HENADZI KILENT/Shutterstock.com, p. 9; Kirill Kukhmar/ITAR-TASS News Agency/Alamy Stock Photo, p. 11; WAYHOME studio/Shutterstock.com, pp. 13, 23 (top left); maja wasowicz/Shutterstock.com, pp. 15, 23 (bottom left); istetiana/Shutterstock.com, p. 17; Iakov Filimonov/Shutterstock.com, pp. 19, 23 (top right); izikMD/Shutterstock.com, p. 21; Ermolaev Alexander/Shutterstock.com, p. 22. Cover: Preto Perola/Shutterstock.com (top); Volosina/Shutterstock.com (bottom).

Main body text set in Mikado a Medium. Typeface provided by HVD Fonts.

Library of Congress Cataloging-in-Publication Data

Names: Taus-Bolstad, Stacy, author.
Title: The story of bread : it starts with wheat / Stacy Taus-Bolstad.
Description: Minneapolis : Lerner Publications, 2022 | Series: Step by step | Includes bibliographical references and index. | Audience: Ages 4–8 | Audience: Grades K–1 | Summary: "Follow the journey from golden wheat fields to fresh-baked bread loaf. Simple text and colorful photos explain this delicious process step by step"— Provided by publisher.
Identifiers: LCCN 2020058583 (print) | LCCN 2020058584 (ebook) | ISBN 9781728428222 (library binding) | ISBN 9781728431673 (paperback) | ISBN 9781728430867 (ebook)
Subjects: LCSH: Bread—Juvenile literature. | Wheat—Processing—Juvenile literature.
Classification: LCC TX769 T3556 2022 (print) | LCC TX769 (ebook) | DDC 641.81/5—dc23

LC record available at https://lccn.loc.gov/2020058583
LC ebook record available at https://lccn.loc.gov/2020058584

Manufactured in the United States of America
1-49359-49463-3/4/2021

Bread is good to eat.
How is it made?

A farmer plants wheat.

The farmer cuts
the wheat.

Machines make flour.

The flour is bagged.

A baker makes dough.

A mixer stirs
the dough.

The dough rises.

The baker shapes loaves.

The loaves are baked.

Time to eat!

Picture Glossary

dough

loaf

mixer

wheat

Learn More

Colella, Jill. *Let's Explore Bread!* Minneapolis: Lerner Publications, 2020.

Nelson, Penelope. *From Wheat to Bread*. Minneapolis: Jump!, 2021.

Ridley, Sarah. *Seeds to Bread.* New York: Crabtree, 2019.

Index